The Harlem Globetrotters

Clown Princes of Basketball

D1373204

by Robbie Butler

Reading Consultant:
Timothy Rasinski, Ph.D.
Professor of Reading Education
Kent State University

Red Brick™ Learning

tPublished by Red Brick™ Learning
7825 Telegraph Road, Bloomington, Minnesota 55438
http://www.redbricklearning.com

Library of Congress Cataloging-in-Publication Data
Butler, Robbie. 1949-
    The Harlem Globetrotters: clown princes of basketball/by Robbie Butler.
    p. cm.
    Includes bibliographic references (p. 62) and index.
    Summary: Relates the story of the Harlem Globetrotters basketball team,
from their founding to the present, highlighting notable players as well as the
humanitarian efforts of the Globetrotter organization.
    ISBN-13: 978-0-7368-4001-9 (hard)
    ISBN-10: 0-7368-4001-X (hard)
    ISBN-13: 978-0-7368-9501-9 (pbk.)
    ISBN-10: 0-7368-9501-9 (pbk.)
    1. Harlem Globetrotters—Juvenile literature. [1. Harlem Globetrotters.
2. Basketball.] I. Title.
GV885.52.N38 B88 2001
796.323'64'097471—dc21

                                                                2001002930

Created by Kent Publishing Services, Inc.
Designed by Signature Design Group, Inc.

Photo Credits:
Cover, pages 4, 14, 57, Sol Tucker/ECA Magazines; pages 6, 11, 12, 17, 21, 24,
27, 29, 31, 35, 38, Bettmann/Corbis; page 19, Charles A. Harris/Corbis; pages
22, 32, 36–37, AP Laserphoto; page 33, Henry Diltz/Corbis; pages 41, 43, UPI
Photo Service; page 44, Al Goldis/AP Photo; page 46, Ken Levine/Allsport; page
51, Hulton-Deutsch Collection/Corbis; page 53, Walter Dhladhla, AFP/Corbis;
page 54, Reuters NewMedia Inc./Corbis

Printed in the United States of America.

Table of Contents

— CHAPTER 1 —

The Start of Basketball

Do you like to see soaring slam dunks? How about half-court shots that hit nothing but net? Do you like to laugh out loud? Then you'll love the Harlem Globetrotters!

The Globetrotter's famous water-toss routine

Where Michael Got His Game

Superstar Michael Jordan has an amazing style of basketball. Where did it come from? A few years ago, one sportswriter gave this opinion: "There might have been no Michael Jordan without the Globetrotters and their game of risk and flash."

The sportswriter was referring to the Harlem Globetrotters. Also called the Globies or Trotters, the Globetrotters play a unique style of basketball. Some people call them artists. Others call them clowns. Watch them play, and you will see they are both.

The Globies can rattle the rim and tickle your funny bone. But they are more than just showmen. The Globies travel the world to inspire, entertain, and educate people.

The Globetrotters are an important part of the rich history of basketball—a game that began more than 100 years ago.

---

risk: the chance of losing or failing
showman: a person who performs in an exciting way
inspire: to encourage someone to do something

Basketball Starts Slowly

Basketball was invented in 1891 by a Canadian, James A. Naismith. This young minister was teaching physical education at a YMCA in Springfield, Massachusetts. He wanted to invent a game that would be good for the physical and spiritual fitness of young people. So he nailed two peach baskets to the gym walls and created the first rules for basketball.

Basketball gradually became more popular and spread across the country. In the early days, the style of play was very controlled and slow. There were no slam dunks or fast breaks. The jump shot was not even invented yet!

In the 1920s, a new style began to develop. It did not develop in the YMCAs, however. This new style was born in a neighborhood in New York City called Harlem. But it was not the Harlem Globetrotters who invented it!

YMCA: Young Men's Christian Association
spiritual: to do with the soul and not with physical things

A Few of James Naismith's 13 Rules for Basketball

Dr. James Naismith

A player cannot run with the ball, but must throw it from the spot where he catches it.

No shouldering, holding, pushing, tripping, or striking of an opponent will be allowed.

A foul is striking at the ball with a fist.

A goal shall be made when the ball is thrown or batted from the ground into the basket and stays there.

The Harlem Rens Speed Things Up

In 1923, a team called the Harlem Renaissance was formed. People called them the Rens. Their name came from the dance hall where they played in Harlem.

Many people agree that the Rens were the best basketball team at that time. They changed basketball to a fast, exciting game, with quick passing and tough defense.

The Rens were an all-black team. Segregation and racism kept African Americans and whites from playing on the same team. In fact, it was not until the 1950s that an African American played in the National Basketball Association (NBA).

There were only a few teams that could challenge the Rens. One team was the Original Celtics. During the 1926-27 season, the Rens split a six-game series with the Celtics.

---

renaissance: a rebirth
segregation: the act of keeping groups of people apart
racism: an idea that one race of people is better than another

During the next four years, the Rens put together a record of 473 wins and 99 losses. This included an unbeaten string of 88 straight games.

Despite the problem of segregation, the Rens proved that African Americans could play, coach, and operate an exciting and successful basketball team. They helped pave the way for the Harlem Globetrotters.

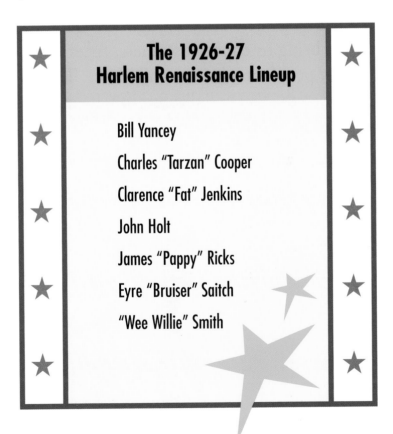

The 1926-27 Harlem Renaissance Lineup

Bill Yancey

Charles "Tarzan" Cooper

Clarence "Fat" Jenkins

John Holt

James "Pappy" Ricks

Eyre "Bruiser" Saitch

"Wee Willie" Smith

The Savoy Big Five

In the 1920s, young people liked a type of music called big band music. These big bands often played in large ballrooms. People paid to hear the bands and to dance. Also at this time, the game of basketball was becoming popular.

This gave ballroom owners an idea. They would try to boost their dance business with basketball games. They thought the games might bring in dance customers. After the games, people might stay and dance. The owner of the Savoy Ballroom in Chicago decided to try this.

People gather outside the Savoy Ballroom.

In 1926, 24-year-old Abe Saperstein started a basketball team. He was looking for a place where his team could play. The Savoy Ballroom hired them. The team became the Savoy Big Five. But the games did not boost business at the Savoy. So the ballroom dropped the team.

Playing on the Road

Saperstein did not give up. He changed the team to a touring team. Three players from the Savoy Big Five formed the core of the new team. This team played their first game in Hinckley, Illinois, on January 7, 1927. Three hundred people paid to see the game.

In their early days, the whole team crammed into Saperstein's Model T Ford to get to their games. Saperstein coached the team and sometimes played.

Abe Saperstein, founder of the Globetrotters

touring: traveling from place to place to perform

The team became successful touring the Midwest. Saperstein changed their name to the Harlem Globetrotters. He thought using the name Harlem would attract more people to the games. Also, the name Globetrotters highlighted that the team travelled to play.

In 1939, the Globetrotters made it to their first professional basketball championship playoffs. The Rens beat them in the semifinal game.

In one game that season, the Globetrotters were winning big. The score was 112-5. The Trotters knew they would win. So the players started to clown around. The crowd loved it! Saperstein then told them to clown away. The "Clown Princes of Basketball" were born!

---

semifinal: coming just before the final game or match

CHAPTER 2

The Clown Princes of Basketball

What comes to mind when you hear the phrase "clown prince"? What do you think a clown prince is? See if some of these Globetrotters match your idea of a clown, a prince, or both.

The Globetrotters are famous for making behind-the-back shots.

World Basketball Champions

Abe Saperstein formed the Harlem Globetrotters to be a serious basketball team. He recruited the best players he could find. He wanted his team to become the best basketball team in the world.

For 12 years, the Globetrotters took on any team that would play them. They beat just about all of them. Then finally in 1940, the Globetrotters won the World Basketball Championship by defeating the Chicago Bruins. Saperstein had reached his goal. The Globetrotters had become the best basketball team in the world.

It wasn't winning a world championship that made them famous, however. It was their clowning around during games that made them so popular.

---

recruit: to hire new members

Inman Jackson

As early as 1929, some Globetrotters began to perform amazing stunts. Inman Jackson was one of these players. Jackson also had a terrific sense of humor. He was the first person to make laughter part of the Globetrotter game plan.

The Globetrotters had become almost too good. Fans and even the Trotters themselves were becoming bored during games. Some teams even stopped inviting them back to play again. Who wanted to get beaten 112-5? So Jackson and his teammates began to clown around and perform tricks.

The Globies began to spin the ball on their fingers during games—something fans had never seen before. They made baskets by bouncing the ball off their heads. They would even line up in a football formation. One player would snap the ball to Jackson, who would drop-kick it into the basket! The crowd loved it.

The Globetrotters could still play championship basketball. But now they were becoming showmen as well.

Inman Jackson

Reece "Goose" Tatum

The popularity of the Globetrotters' new style of play grew. In 1942, Saperstein hired a player who would take this clowning to a new level. Reece Tatum brought to the Globetrotters incredible basketball skills and hilarious comic routines.

Tatum had huge hands and a very long neck and arms. His "wing span" was 7 feet (2.1 meters)! Tatum looked awkward when he caught a ball. For these reasons, people gave him the nickname "Goose."

Goose developed several routines the team still uses today. One of these was "the swing." To do the swing, Goose would whirl the ball around his hips to confuse defenders.

Another trick was "the roll." For this move, Goose would fake a pass in one direction and roll the ball to a teammate in the other.

---

hilarious: very funny
comic: funny or amusing
routine: a play done over and over

Goose's most famous move made it to the NBA! He would hold the ball in one hand above his head when passing or shooting his hook shot. Many basketball greats copied this move. They include such legends as Wilt Chamberlain, Connie Hawkins, Julius Erving, and Michael Jordan.

Reece Tatum

Meadow George Lemon, III

The tradition of clown princes continued into the 1950s. Another great showman, Robert "Showboat" Hall, was a passing and ball-handling wizard. People said Hall was so quick, he could pull the ball out of thin air—and make it disappear.

In 1954, Showboat Hall became ill. But another player quickly filled his role. His name was Meadow George Lemon, III.

Have you ever heard someone say they did something "for a lark"? The phrase means just for fun—with maybe a little harmless mischief mixed in. That was how Meadow played basketball and how he earned his nickname, "Meadowlark."

Meadowlark Lemon quickly became a fan favorite. He created many famous Trotter routines that you can still see today. These include the basketball-medicine ball switch and the rubber-banded foul shot.

---

tradition: a custom, idea, or belief that is repeated
mischief: a playful trick or prank

Meadowlark also was the first to make fans scream with the "confetti toss." Meadowlark would grab a bucket that everyone thought was filled with water and begin to chase another player. Then he would suddenly heave the bucket into the stands. The crowd would scream as confetti floated down on them.

Meadowlark wore the Globetrotter red, white, and blue for 24 years. The tricks he invented still make fans laugh today.

Meadow George Lemon, III

---

confetti: tiny bits of paper

Hubert "Geese" Ausbie

Hubert "Geese" Ausbie also played the clown prince role. In 1961, Ausbie attended a Globetrotter tryout camp. The competition included more than 500 players from around the country. Ausbie made the team. He even turned down a pro baseball contract to put on a Globetrotter uniform.

Hubert "Geese" Ausbie

A quiet gentleman off the court, Geese was a hilarious showman on the court. Like Meadowlark, he carried on the Globetrotter tradition for 24 years, from 1961-1985.

Great Players on a Great Team

With all the clowning around, it's easy to forget that the Globetrotters are a first-rate basketball team. In 1940, the Globies started a tradition of playing college all-star teams. They have won most of those games. In 1999, they beat a college all-star team that sent six players to the NBA.

It takes great players to be a great team. The Globetrotters have been loaded with the best. In the next chapter, you'll meet some of the greatest Globetrotter players of all time.

Clowning around on a playground in Chicago, 1960

CHAPTER 3

Globetrotter Greats

What do you think makes a basketball player great? What qualities does a player need to be better than the rest? The Globetrotter players in this chapter are considered to be some of the greatest. See if you agree.

Excellent Showmen and Athletes

The Globetrotters have been around for a long time. In fact, in 2001, the Globetrotters held their 75th anniversary celebration.

Many players have worn the red, white, and blue-spangled jerseys of the Harlem Globetrotters over this time. All have been excellent basketball players. Some have been expert showmen as well. A few of those players have left a mark on the game that may never be erased.

---

spangled: covered with small, shiny objects

Marques Haynes

In the 1940s and 1950s, Marques Haynes and Reece "Goose" Tatum teamed up on a memorable Globetrotter team. Goose provided the clowning and Haynes provided pure, rare athletic talent.

Some call Haynes the most gifted dribbler of all time. Haynes helped his high school team win the Oklahoma state championship in 1942. Haynes next played with the all-black Langston University team. With Haynes, that team had a four-year record of 112-3 and won two conference titles. Haynes also led Langston to a rare victory over the touring Harlem Globetrotters.

After college, Haynes joined the Trotters. He played on and off for them for three decades. He once left the team to form his own team with Goose Tatum. They called their team the Harlem Magicians.

---

conference: a group of athletic teams
decade: 10 years

Haynes played basketball for more than 40 years. During that time he logged more games (more than 12,000), more miles (more than 4 million—6.4 million kilometers), and more places (every U.S. state, 97 countries, and six continents) than any other basketball player in history.

Haynes also was the first Globetrotter to be inducted into the Naismith Memorial Basketball Hall of Fame.

Marques Haynes

log: to record or have to one's credit
induct: to formally bring into a club

Wilt "The Stilt" Chamberlain

In 75 years, the Harlem Globetrotters have retired only three jersey numbers. This honor went to Wilt Chamberlain (#13), Marques Haynes (#20), and Meadowlark Lemon (#36). Wilt Chamberlain's was the first to be retired.

As a 7-foot-1-inch center, Chamberlain began his professional career with the Globetrotters in 1958. He played for one year and then joined the NBA.

During his NBA career, Chamberlain set many records. Some of those records still stand today. In his third year, he averaged an amazing 50 points per game. He once scored 100 points in a game against the New York Knicks. He grabbed 23,924 rebounds (22.9 per game) during his career. That NBA record still stands today. He also never fouled out during his 1,045 NBA games.

---

retire: to never use again

Wilt Chamberlain

Connie "the Hawk" Hawkins

Connie Hawkins may be the greatest legend to ever come out of the playground courts of New York City. He dazzled Globetrotter fans during the early 1960s.

Hawkins could dribble, pass, and leap better than anyone else ever had. Many say his style of playing paved the way for the high-flying acts of Julius Erving and Michael Jordan.

Hawkins joined the American Basketball Association (ABA) after playing for the Globetrotters. He later joined the NBA.

During his seven years in the NBA, Hawkins made the All-Star team four times. He appeared in 511 career NBA games (16.6 points per game) and 138 ABA games (28.2 points per game). He now works for the NBA's Phoenix Suns.

---

dazzle: to impress or amaze
pave: to lead

Connie Hawkins

Fred "Curly" Neal

Curly Neal is another of the great dribblers in basketball history. Also an excellent shooter, he regularly swished the ball from beyond mid-court.

Neal, a 6-foot-1-inch guard, was a key member of the Globetrotters from 1963 to 1985. He played over 6,000 games in 97 countries. He still serves as an "Ambassador of Goodwill" for the team. He also works for the NBA's Orlando Magic basketball team.

Fred Neal

ambassador: a person who represents an organization

Lynette Woodard

Lynette Woodard

Lynette Woodard was the first woman to play for the Globetrotters. The 6-foot guard joined the team in 1985. Woodard played college basketball at the University of Kansas from 1978 to 1981. There she averaged 26.3 points per game and made All-American four times.

Woodard also played for the gold-medal-winning 1984 U.S. Olympic team. In 1987, she left the Globetrotters to play for professional teams in Italy and Japan.

Junius Kellogg

Junius Kellogg, a 6-foot-10-inch center, was the first African American to play at Manhattan College in New York. His honesty helped end a scandal at the college. Kellogg reported that a gambler had asked him to fix a game. He refused to cheat, however, and fans across the nation called him a hero.

After college in 1953, Kellogg signed with the Globetrotters. Tragically, he was disabled in a car crash in 1954. Still, he continued to contribute to basketball. Kellogg helped start the National Wheelchair Basketball Association. In 1964, he won a gold medal at the Paralympics.

---

scandal: something that causes shame or disgrace
gambler: a person who bets money on the result of a game
fix: to attempt to change the result of a game

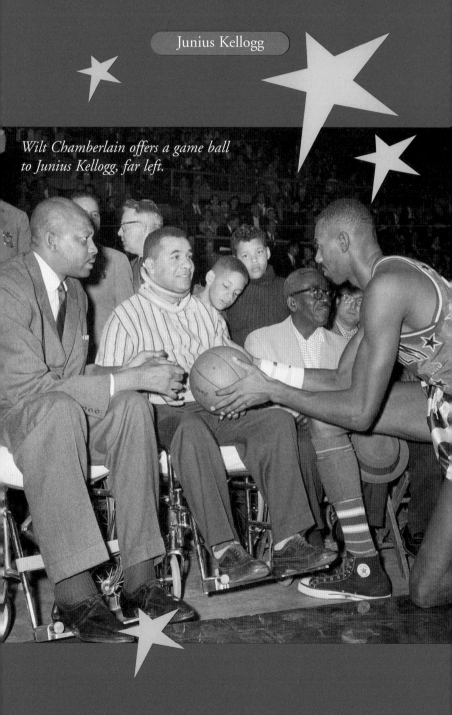

Wilt Chamberlain offers a game ball to Junius Kellogg, far left.

Michael "Wild Thing" Wilson

Globetrotter Michael Wilson is known for his seemingly effortless leaping ability. Nicknamed "Wild Thing," he holds the world record for the slam dunk. The 6-foot-6-inch Wilson dunked a basketball on a 12-foot goal. An official basketball goal is 10 feet. This record was officially recognized by the Guinness Book of World Records. Wilson is one of the most exciting leapers and high-flying dunkers in team history.

The Greatest of Them All?

The Globetrotters have had many great players over the past 75 years. But one person just may be the greatest Globetrotter of them all. This former player now owns the team. He stepped in to save the Globetrotters when they were struggling to survive. His nickname is "Young Squirrel." Can you guess why his teammates gave him this name?

The Globetrotters were the first athletic team to be honored with a star in the world famous Hollywood Walk of Fame.

Mannie Jackson, current owner of the Globetrotters

Chapter 4

Young Squirrel

What do you think it means to say a person has overcome the odds to succeed? What kind of person do you think can do this? Do you know someone who has overcome the odds?

Mr. Basketball

The man who owns and runs the Harlem Globetrotters has come a long way himself. Mannie Jackson was born in a railroad boxcar in Illmo, Missouri. He grew up in Edwardsville, Illinois, where he learned to play and love the game of basketball.

In high school, Jackson earned high honors for his basketball skills. He was named a high school All-American, as well as "Mr. Basketball" and "Player of the Year" in Illinois. At the University of Illinois, he became the school's first African American All-American and captain of the team.

---

boxcar: a railroad car shaped like a box or rectangle

Mannie the Globetrotter

Jackson played for the Globetrotters during the 1960s. He was known for his lightning quick speed and his 43-inch (109-centimeter) vertical leap. Because of his endless energy, Meadowlark Lemon nicknamed him "Young Squirrel."

Young Squirrel is now the owner and chairman of the Harlem Globetrotters. Some might even call him the man who saved the Trotters.

In 1993, the Globetrotters were facing bankruptcy. But Jackson saw an opportunity to turn the business around. He put together a group of investors to buy it. They purchased the team for $5.5 million. Today, the Globetrotters are worth more than $50 million. Jackson is the first African American and former player to own a sports and entertainment team.

---

chairman: a person in charge of a company
bankruptcy: when a person or company is not able to pay its debts
investor: a person who lends money hoping to make a profit

Mannie Jackson presents track star Jackie Joyner-Kersee with her own Globetrotter jersey in 1999. Joyner-Kersee is an honorary Harlem Globetrotter.

Preparing for the Future

A young squirrel seldom sits still. Jackson isn't resting on his success either. He has a lot of new ideas about where he wants the Globetrotters to be in the future.

Jackson remembers the roots of the Globetrotters. He knows that they were formed to be a competitive, championship team. Yet he also knows that fans love them for entertaining and clowning around. Nonetheless, Jackson wants his team to be respected as one of the best in the world.

In order for the Globetrotters to be both the best team and the best entertainers, Jackson has made some changes. Following in Abe Saperstein's footsteps, he is trying to recruit the best basketball players. He also is trying to play the best teams in the world.

Curley "Boo" Johnson's dribbling skills helped him become a Globetrotter entertainer.

Trying Out for the Trotters

The Globetrotters hold tryouts each year.
They decide who makes the team based
totally on each player's basketball skills. The
tricks will come later. Jackson believes that
good basketball players can learn to become
entertaining Globetrotters. He should know.
He was both.

Playing the Best

Jackson also wants his players to challenge the best teams in the world. During the 2000-2001 season, the Globetrotters beat Metro State College of Denver—the National Collegiate Athletic Association (NCAA) Division II national champion.

A few days after the Metro State game, the Trotters took on Michigan State, the Division I national champs. The game went down to the wire. Finally, Michigan State defeated the Globetrotters 72-68. That loss broke the Globetrotters 1,270-game win streak.

The Ultimate Challenge Team

Jackson would like the Globetrotters to be the ultimate challenge team. Currently, the Globetrotters have three teams that tour. He would like to pick the best players from the three teams. These players would then challenge any team that would face them—just as Saperstein's Globetrotters did.

Jackson dreams of the day when he can schedule a game each year with the NBA champion, the NCAA champion, and the champion of every country that plays good basketball. He wants to be one of the top 20 teams in the world.

Can Jackson get all these teams to agree to play the Globies? Who knows. But Young Squirrel recently told reporters, "We're ready to play. That's the Globetrotter way."

---

ultimate: the greatest possible

Michigan State's Jason Richardson and Globetrotter Wayne Turner hit the floor for a loose ball.

Chapter 5

Ambassadors of Goodwill

The Globetrotters are great athletes and entertainers. They have fans around the world. Does being famous and well liked give them any special opportunities or duties?

Curly Johnson teaches a fan a trick.

Sweet Charity

The word *charity* means "giving help or money to needy people." Another meaning is "goodwill or love towards others." *Charity* also means "understanding or tolerance for those who are different."

The Harlem Globetrotters practice all these types of charity. People see the Globetrotters as role models both on and off the court. They have become America's Ambassadors of Goodwill.

The Globetrotters really have two missions. One is to entertain with their amazing basketball skills and humor. The other is to promote peace and goodwill around the world.

Mannie Jackson and his team have helped to break down barriers of poverty and hatred. They do this through charity, and also by adding a few special "players" to their team.

---

tolerance: a willingness to let others have their own beliefs

Give Something Back

Jackson has many daily duties as owner of the Globetrotters. Still, he takes on other jobs as well. Groups around the world ask him to speak. He makes hundreds of speeches every year. He was the main speaker at the first annual Black History Heritage Celebration in 2000.

As well as time, Jackson gives money. Some years ago, he began "give-back initiatives." For one of these, the Jackson family gave $100,000 to Mannie's old school in Edwardsville, Illinois. The Globetrotters organization has donated more than $10 million for youth organizations since 1993.

Send a Kid to See the Trotters

Jackson and local companies join forces and buy Globetrotter game tickets for young people. These girls and boys also attend a pre-game clinic with members of the team.

---

initiative: a first step in bringing something about
clinic: a brief training session

At the clinic, Globetrotter players talk with these young people about self-esteem and education. The young people learn about the value of drug-free, gang-free, and violence-free neighborhoods. They also get to play some ball. That night, the kids watch the greatest basketball show on Earth.

Summer Camps

The Globetrotters hold summer camps for kids in more than 15 U.S. cities. Some families cannot afford to pay camp fees. Their fees are paid for by one of the Globetrotter partners in charity.

At camp, young people aged 6-16 get to work with Globetrotter players and coaches every day for a week. The youngsters sharpen their basketball skills while also working on attitude and leadership. Talk about happy campers!

---

self-esteem: belief in oneself
attitude: a way of acting or behaving

49

Special Recruits

The Globetrotters have recruited some other special people to help them reach their goals. Look at the list of names below. What do you think these people have in common?

Henry Kissinger	Nelson Mandela
Whoopi Goldberg	The Rev. Jesse Jackson
Jackie Joyner-Kersee	Pope John Paul II
Kareem Abdul-Jabbar	Bob Hope

You might answer that each is famous. Each is a success. Each has done a lot of good. Each has a strong character. All these answers are true. But these people also share one more thing. Each is an honorary member of the Harlem Globetrotters.

The Globetrotters honor special people who have become successful. Even more important, these people have done good deeds that have left a lasting mark on the world. Read on to learn more about them.

---

character: personal qualities

Henry Kissinger

In 1976, the Globetrotters named their first honorary member. It was Henry Kissinger. A native of Germany, Kissinger served as the U.S. Secretary of State from 1973-1977. He worked hard to improve U.S. relations with both China and the former Soviet Union. Kissinger also helped end the Vietnam War in 1973. For that, he won a Nobel Peace Prize. Later, he worked for peace in the Middle East.

Henry Kissinger

Nelson Mandela

Nelson Mandela was born in 1918, in South Africa. He grew up to become a fighter against a policy called *apartheid* in that country.

Mandella became a leader of the African National Congress (ANC). He was first jailed in 1962 for rebelling against the government. He was convicted and sentenced to life in prison in 1964.

Jailed for 28 years, Mandela became a symbol for the fight against apartheid. Freed in 1990, he again became leader of the ANC. In 1993, Mandela and then President F.W. de Klerk shared the Nobel Peace Prize. In 1994, South Africa held its first democratic elections. The people elected Mandela as their president.

In 1996, the Globetrotters became the first pro basketball team to play in a free democratic South Africa.

---

apartheid: a policy that denied social, political, and economic rights to non-European people in South Africa

Nelson Mandela

Pope John Paul II

Pope John Paul II is the leader of the Roman Catholic Church. A native of Poland, he has named more African Americans to help lead the Roman Catholic Church than any other pope.

Pope John Paul II is also a globetrotter. He has traveled more than any pope in history. His goodwill missions have taken him to more than 116 countries. He was named an honorary Globetrotter in 2000.

Pope John Paul II

Role Models to Many

The story of the Harlem Globetrotters is about much more than basketball. Role models to many, the Clown Princes of Basketball continue to work their magic both on and off the court.

In 1952, a newspaper writer attended a Globetrotters' game in Cairo, Egypt. After the game, he wrote, "When one laughs, one cannot hate."

That's how Clown Princes become Goodwill Ambassadors. That's also how the Harlem Globetrotters became the most popular sports team in the United States. And that's why the Globetrotters will continue to amaze, entertain, and inspire for years and years to come.

Epilogue

Spreading Hope and Opportunity

The Harlem Globetrotters have come a long way. They began as a poor, struggling team filled with the hope of opportunity. Today, they are a successful team spreading hope and opportunity around the world. Best of all, they are having a blast doing it.

Globie

In 1993, on a Harlem playground, Mannie Jackson signed the contract to buy the Globetrotters. A costumed character with a globe for a head turned up at the signing. Everyone there thought he must be the Globetrotters' mascot. One of the kids called him "Globie." So Jackson gave Globie a job.

---

mascot: a person, animal, or thing thought to bring good luck

Some say Globie was a former basketball player. Others say Globie was a 13-year-old boy who was a fan. One thing we know for sure, Globie today stands for millions of fans around the world.

Globie represents the worldwide family. He is not rich or poor. He is not black or white. He is not young or old. Globie is the spirit of the Globetrotters—on and off the court. He is the feeling that makes people young at heart. He is full of fun and goodwill towards all. He is just like the Harlem Globetrotters.

Globie

Globetrotter Firsts

1927 Before a crowd of 300 in Hinckley, Illinois, the Globetrotters play their first touring game.

1946 The first one-armed basketball star, Boid Bui, joins the Globetrotters. Bui averages 18 points per game.

1950 Former Globetrotter Nathaniel "Sweetwater" Clifton becomes the first African American to play in the National Basketball Association.

1968 The Globetrotters play their first game in Harlem, New York, 41 years after their debut in Hinckley.

---

debut: the first appearance before the public

1982 The Globetrotters become the first (and only) sports team ever to be honored with a star in the famous Hollywood Walk of Fame.

1985 The team signs Lynette Woodard, the first woman ever to play professionally for an all-male team.

1993 Mannie Jackson becomes the first former player and African American to own a sports and entertainment organization.

You can also thank the Globetrotters for:
★ the fast break offense
★ the forward and point guard positions
★ regular use of the slam dunk

---

sign: to enter into an agreement

Glossary

ambassador: a person who represents an organization

apartheid: a policy that denied social, political, and economic rights to non-European people in South Africa

attitude: a way of acting or behaving

bankruptcy: when a person or company is not able to pay its debts

boxcar: a railroad car shaped like a box or rectangle

chairman: a person in charge of a company

character: personal qualities

clinic: a brief training session

comic: funny or amusing

conference: a group of athletic teams

confetti: tiny bits of paper

dazzle: to impress or amaze

debut: the first appearance before the public

decade: 10 years

fix: to attempt to change the result of a game

gambler: a person who bets money on the result of a game

hilarious: very funny

induct: to formally bring into a club

initiative: a first step in bringing something about

inspire: to encourage someone to do something

investor: a person who lends money hoping to make a profit

log: to record or have to one's credit

mascot: a person, animal, or thing thought to bring good luck

mischief: a playful trick or prank

pave: to lead

racism: an idea that one race of people is better than another

recruit: to hire new members

renaissance: a rebirth

retire: to never use again

risk: the chance of losing or failing

routine: a play done over and over

scandal: something that causes shame or disgrace

segregation: the act of keeping groups of people apart

self-esteem: belief in oneself

semifinal: coming just before the final game or match

showman: a person who performs in an exciting way

sign: to enter into an agreement

spangled: covered with small, shiny objects

spiritual: to do with the soul and not with physical things

tolerance: a willingness to let others have their own beliefs

touring: traveling from place to place to perform

tradition: a custom, idea, or belief that is repeated

ultimate: the greatest possible

YMCA: Young Men's Christian Association

Bibliography

Anderson, Dave. *The Story of Basketball.* New York: W. Morrow, 1997.

Gault, Clare and Frank Gault. *The Harlem Globetrotters and Basketball's Funniest Games.* New York: Walker, 1977.

Gutman, Bill. *The Harlem Globetrotters: Basketball's Funniest Team.* Champaign, Ill.: Garrard Publishing Co., 1977.

Stewart, Mark. *Basketball: A History of Hoops.* The Watts History of Sports. New York: Franklin Watts, 1998.

Wilker, Josh. *The Harlem Globetrotters.* African-American Achievers. Broomall, Penn.: Chelsea House, 1997.

Useful Addresses

Harlem Globetrotters
400 E. Van Buren Street
Suite # 300
Phoenix, AZ 85004

Naismith Memorial Basketball Hall of Fame
1150 West Columbus Avenue
Springfield, MA 01105

Internet Sites

FactHound offers a safe, fun way to find
Internet sites related to this book. All of the
sites on FactHound have been
researched by our staff.

Here's how:

Visit *www.facthound.com*

FactHound will fetch the best sites for you!

Index